MAY YOUR JOURNEY BE OUR

Joys and Sorrows

Text & Illustrations
By Tom Dunnington

WHAT LIFE
MEANS TO US
IS DETERMINED
NOT SO MUCH BY
WHAT LIFE BRINGS TO US
AS BY THE ATTITUDE
WE BRING TO LIFE.
Dr. L. L. Dunnington

In appreciation of my father, Dr. Lewis Leroy Dunnington, my first teacher.

Neither Joy nor Sorrow is forever.
They are ports of call on our soul's journey.

Transformation is the rearrangement of our pieces into something more beautiful.

Our Joys and Sorrows provide the
energy for our soul's growth.

There is nothing quite as lonely as Sorrow
And nothing as overflowing as Joy.

HOPE is the eternal breath of
Spirit,
breathing in and out of US, daily.

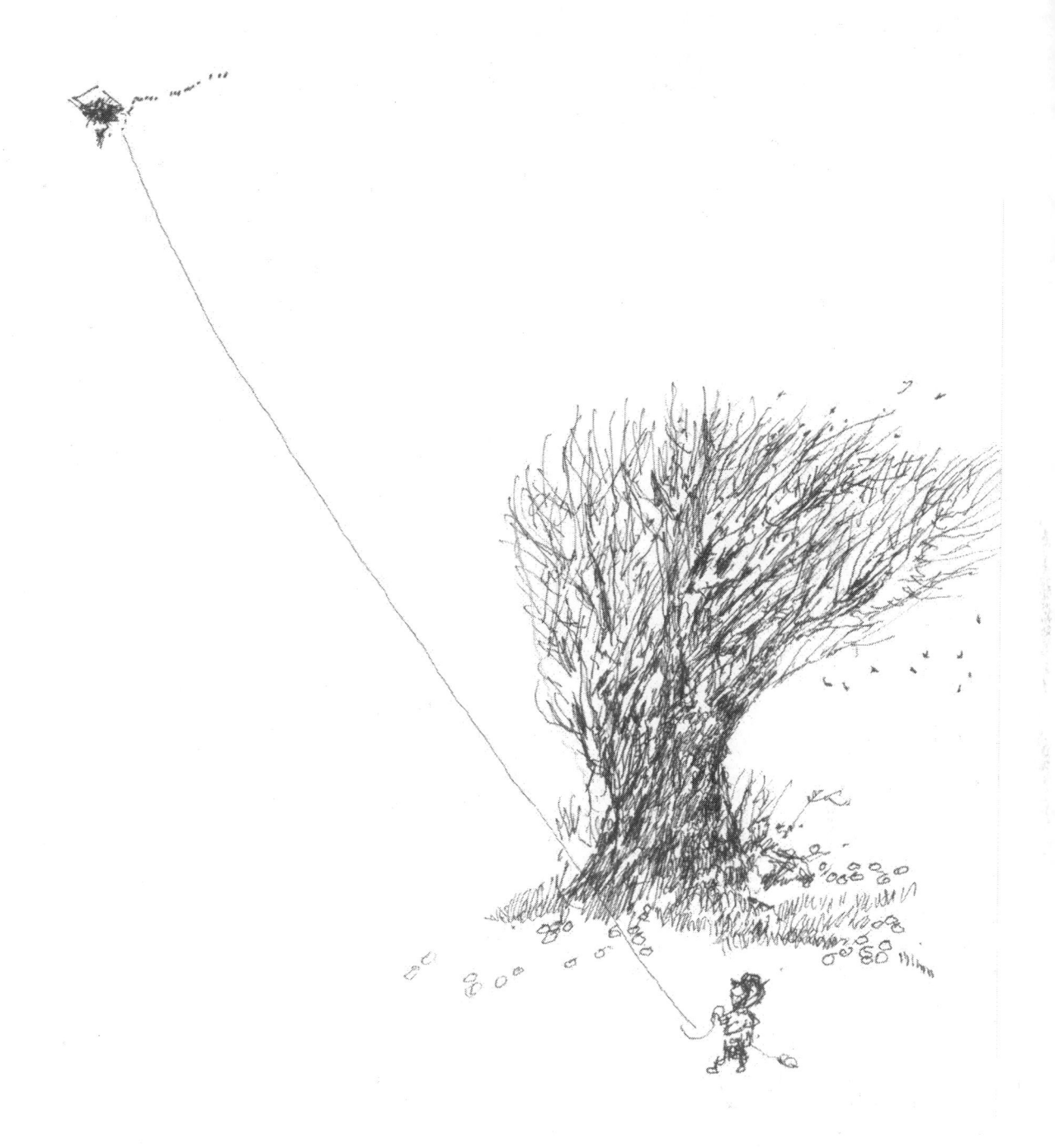

Sorrow is just the residue
of Great Joy.

Sorrow is not eternal.

Joy is not eternal.

Love is eternal.

In the winter of my Sorrow,
I remember the summer of my Joy.

*My Joys are the sails of my ship.
My Sorrows are the wind.*

Your words dress
my world in new
garments.

Joy is available as an alternative to despair.

The Joys and Sorrows of our lives are influenced by our expectations.

I have found many Joys
through tears of Sorrow.

Getting there may be more important than your destination.

Sorrow wants to fill every empty place in your soul.
Fill it, instead, with Joy.

There is plenty to go around.

It is important to own our feelings of pain or loss and it is equally important not to let those feelings own us.

Anger, Hate, Joy or Sorrow
stay with us
for as long as we give them a home.

There is a presence that visits me
in my sorrow and is helping me
find my way back to Joy.

My experiences of Joy or Sorrow
often reflect my commitment to life.

Joy and Sorrow are bites of the same fruit.

My Joy is almost blinding.
I'm thankful for my ability to feel.

Love is the only thing that can change our Joys and Sorrows into the music of our lives.

Spirit is the Force that can transform Joy or Sorrow into Wisdom and Love.

Place your grief on the altar of your beloved and somehow manage to carry on.

Love is the only container large enough to hold our Joys and Sorrows.

Joy is so much more than feeling good. It is the soul rejoicing.

Laughing or weeping, it's all part of growth.

Sometimes there's only room for Sorrow
on my table,
then all I can do is endure.
Sometimes there's only room for Joy
and then I dance.

*No matter how overcast the night sky is,
the stars are always there.*

Our Joys and Sorrows reflect our expectations.

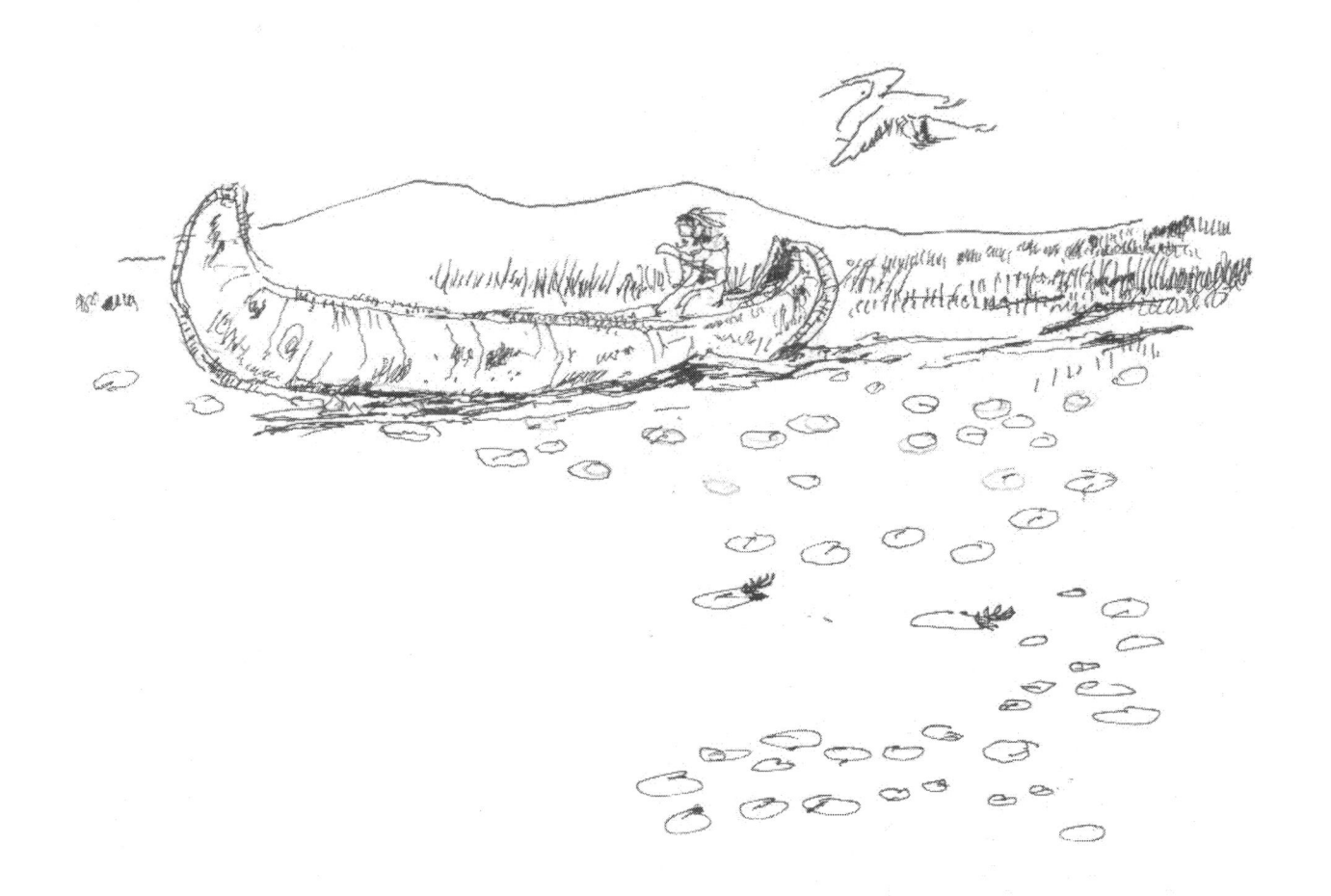

Love is the only thing strong enough to endure your rediscovery of Self.

In the grief you must endure, may
you discover the treasure that is You.

When I examine my Joys and
Sorrows I often find Wisdom.

May you find the Joy imbedded in this day.

My Joy can never be extinguished.
It rises and falls but it is ever present.

I wonder if Joy and Sorrow ever
trade places.

It is easy to think of Joys and Sorrows as punishments or rewards, as success or failures.
They are neither---
they are milestones in our life's journey.

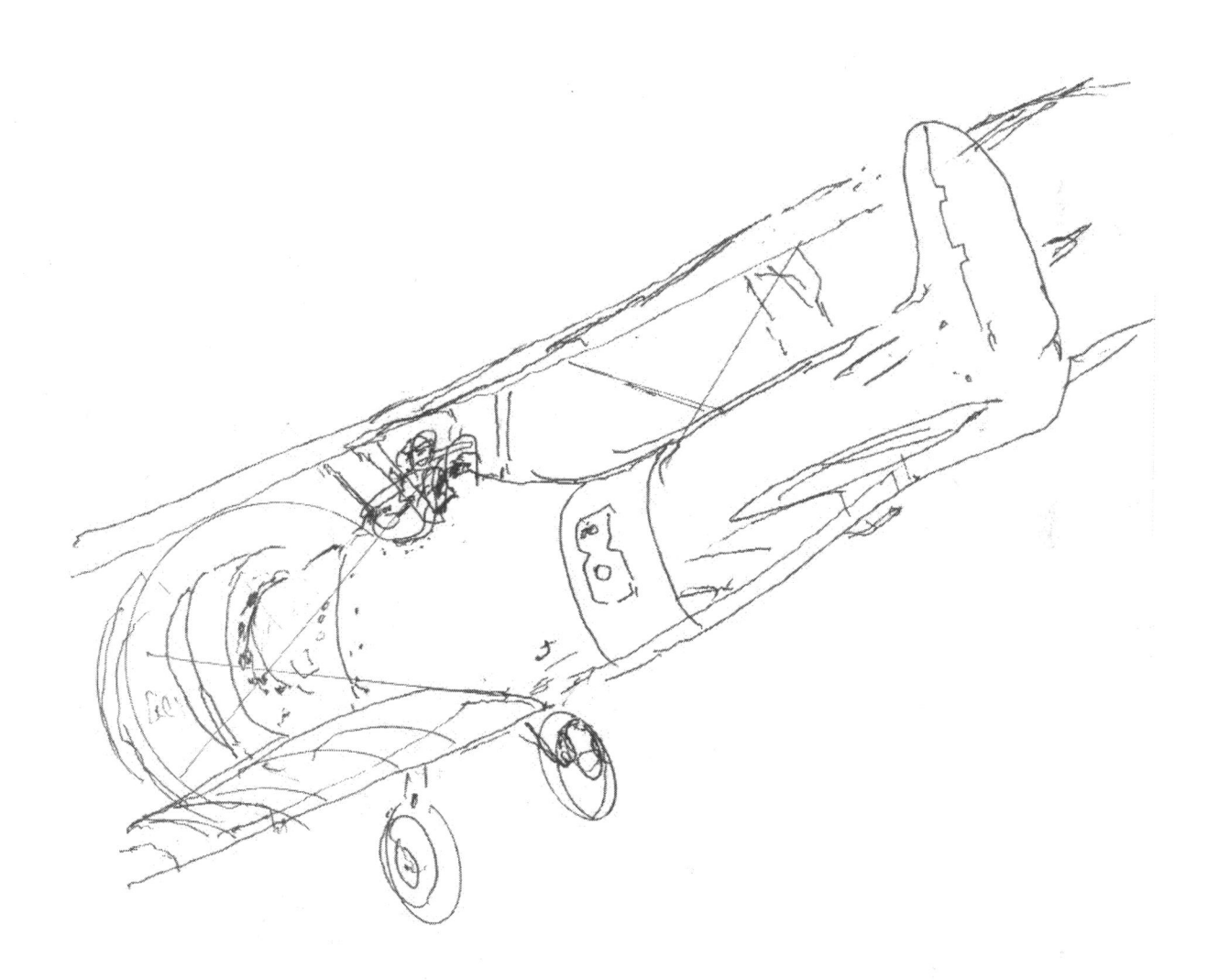

In the winter of my Sorrow,
I remember the summer of my Joy.

It is important to recognize the difference between Sorrow thrust upon us and Sorrow we have chosen.

The Journey from Sorrow back to Joy
always leaves us enriched.

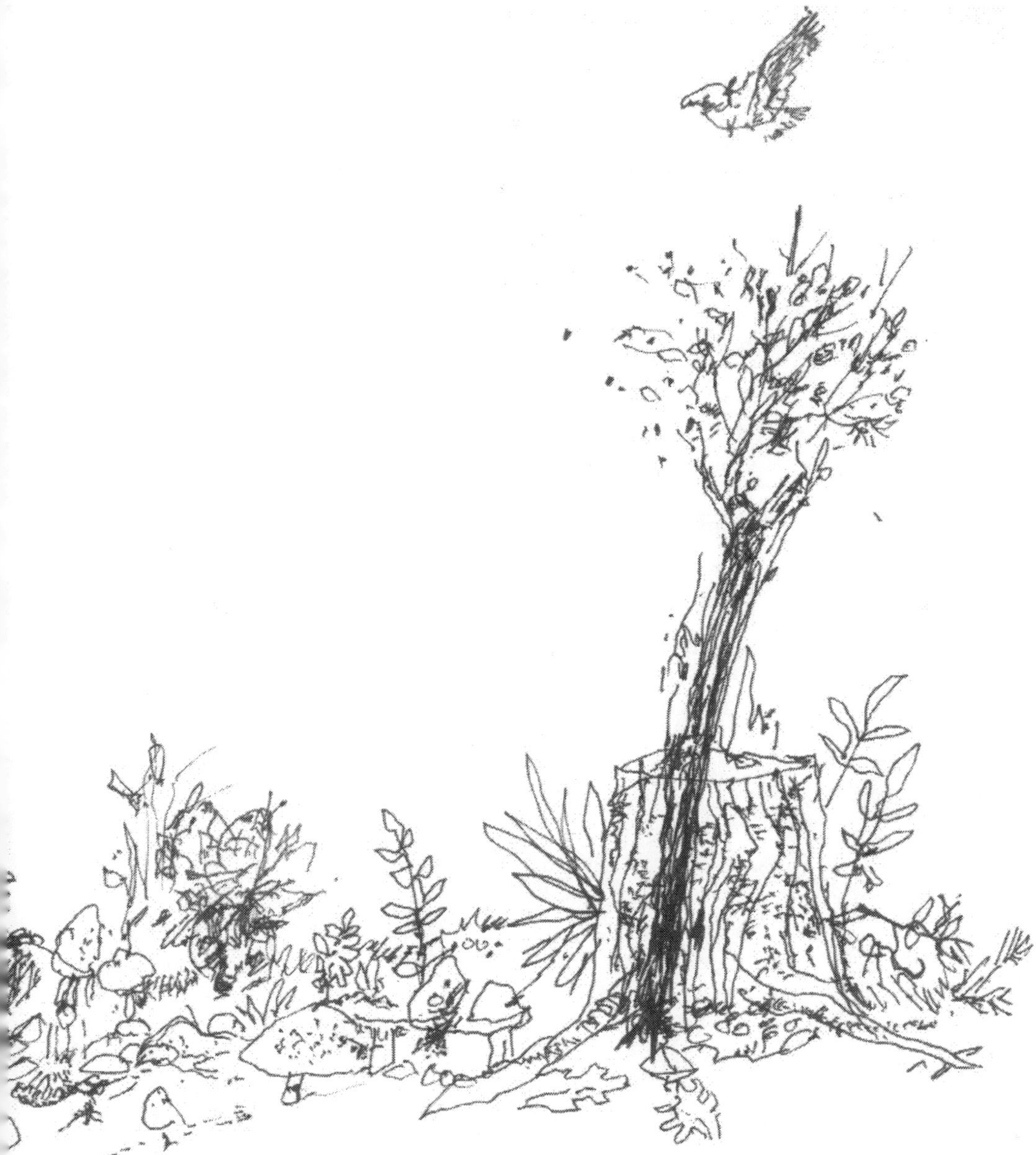

Sorrow is the sound of a tear rolling down your cheek.

Love is the creator of our greatest Joy.
Sorrow is its absence.

The feeling of Joy and the healing of Sorrow
begin with forgiveness.

While getting through your Joys and Sorrows you may find yourself.

Made in the USA
Charleston, SC
19 October 2010